chool

STRAIGHT IS A LINE

a book about lines

by Sharon Lerner

Lerner Publications Company
Minneapolis, Minnesota

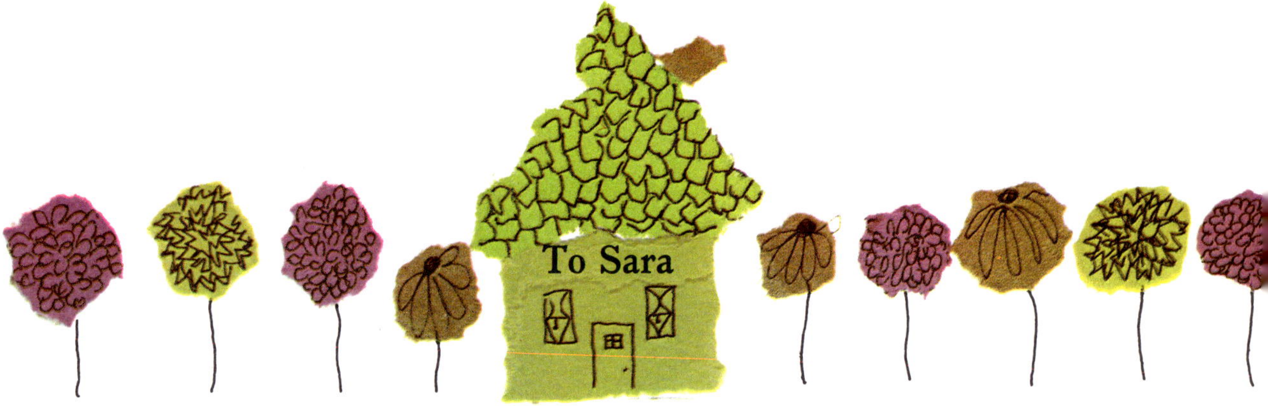

Manufactured in the United States of America. Published simultaneously in Canada by J. M. Dent & Sons Ltd., Don Mills, Ontario.

Standard Book Number: 8225-0273-9
Library of Congress Catalog Card Number: 71-91669

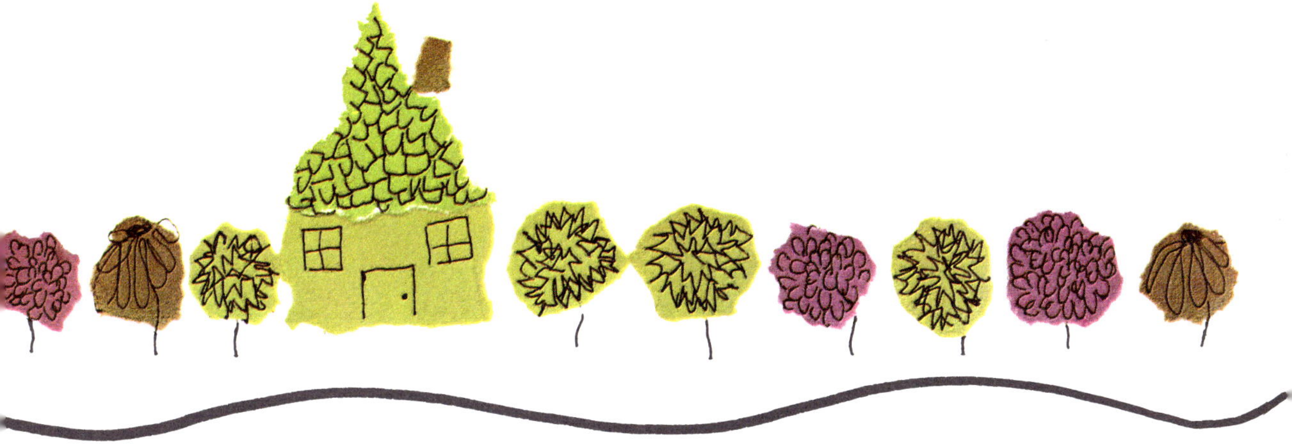

A line is the link from one point to another.
Some lines are straight and others are curved.
The path in front of one house is a straight line.
The path in front of the other house is a curved line.

There are many different straight lines.

This is a vertical line.
Vertical lines go up and down.

This is a horizontal line.
Horizontal lines run across.

These are parallel lines.
They run beside each other,
but they never meet.

This is a slanted line.
It crosses the page at an angle.

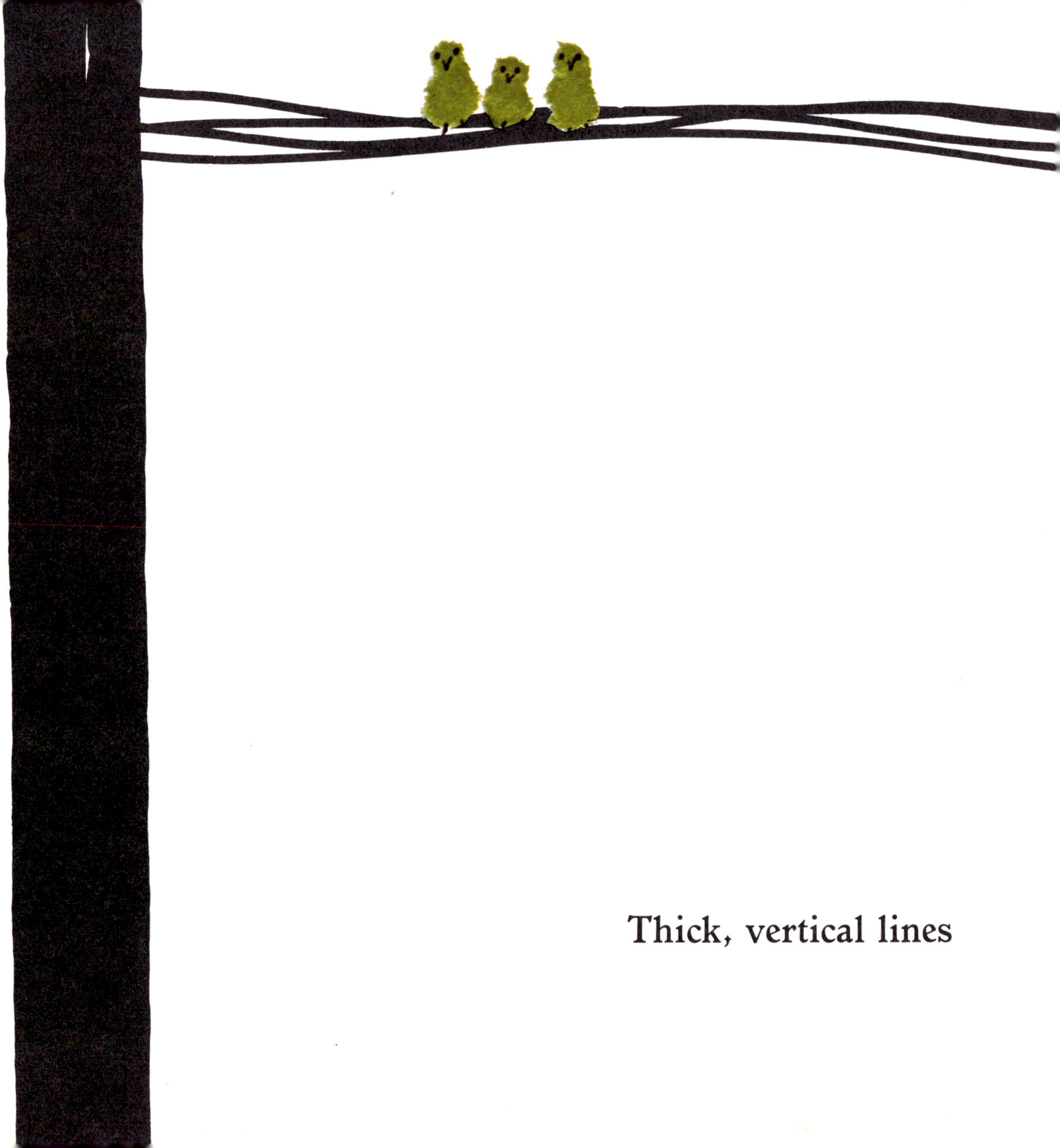

Thick, vertical lines

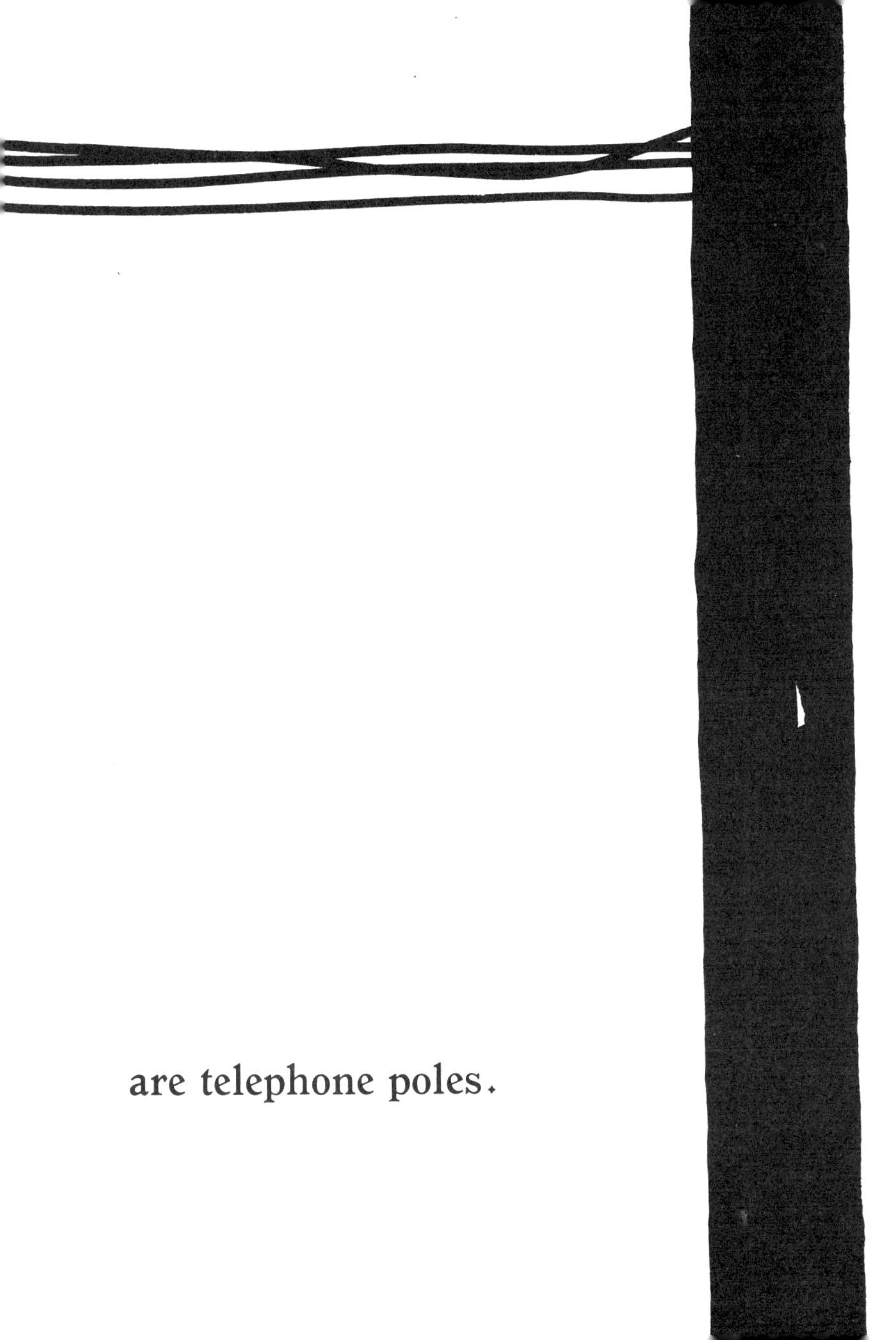

are telephone poles.

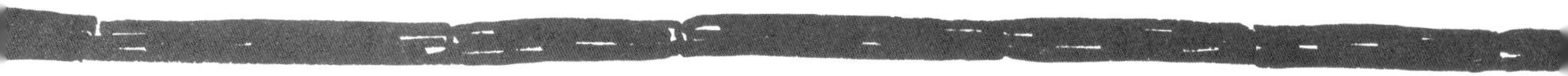

A thin, horizontal line is a fishing pole.

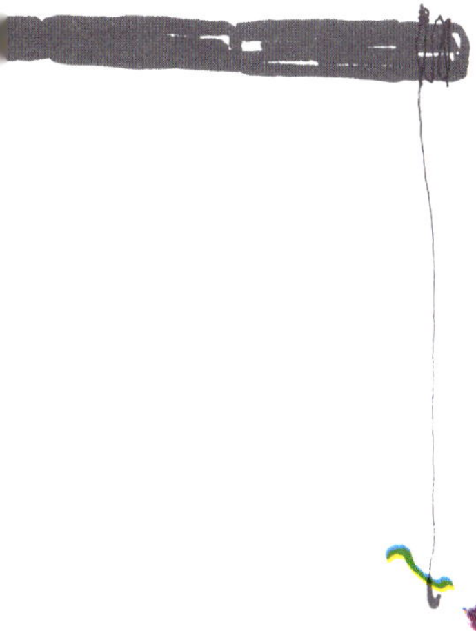

A very thin line is a string to catch a fish.

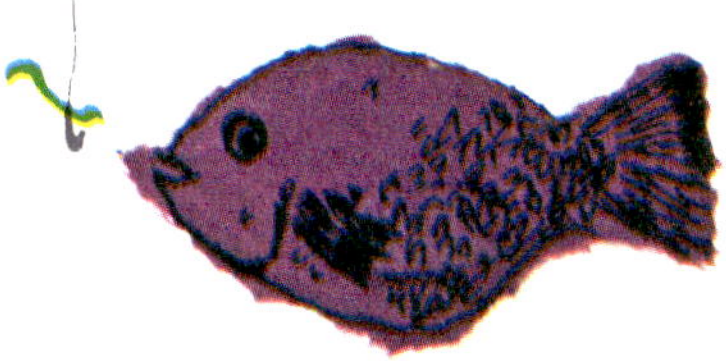

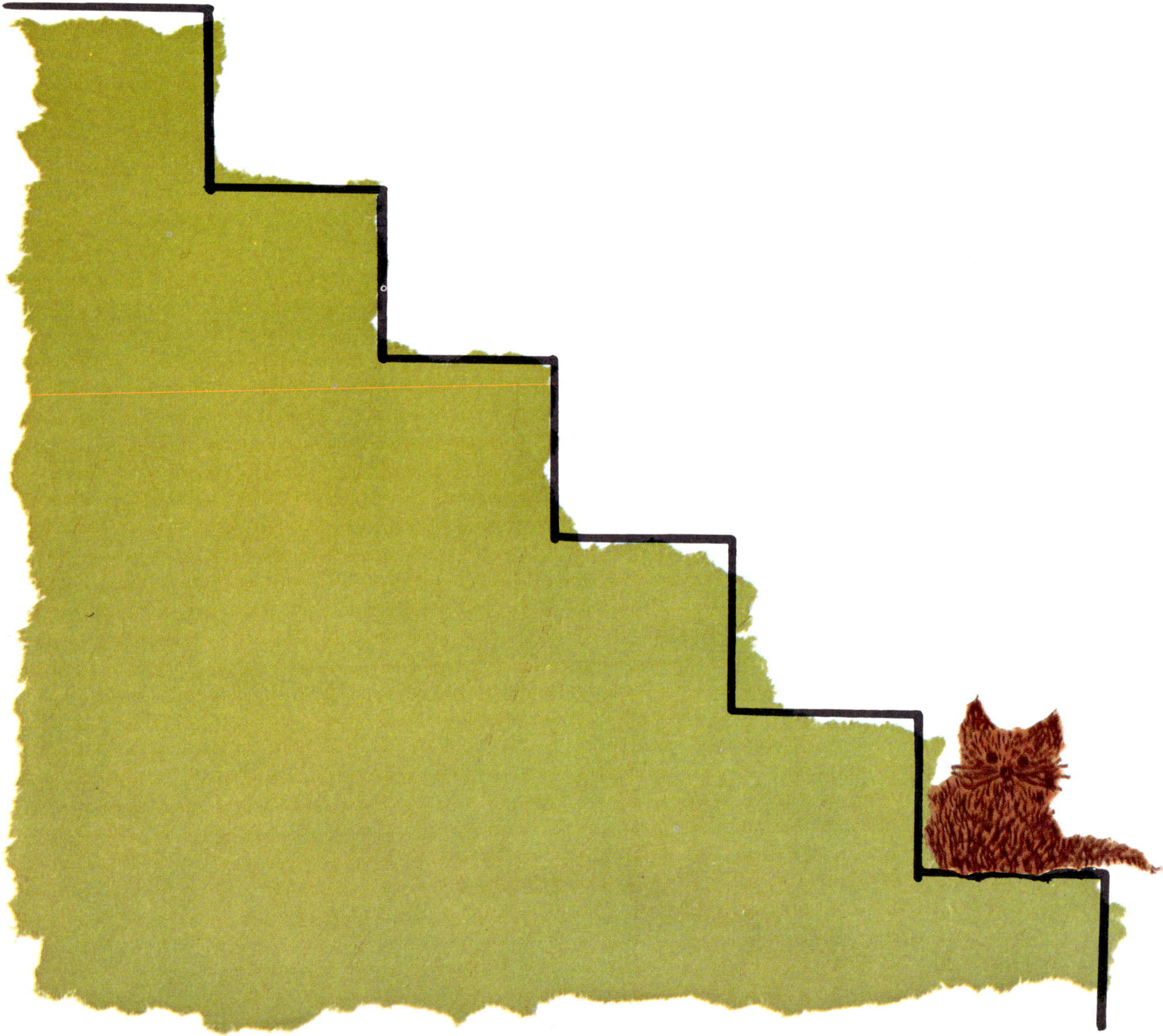

Stairs are made of both horizontal and vertical lines.

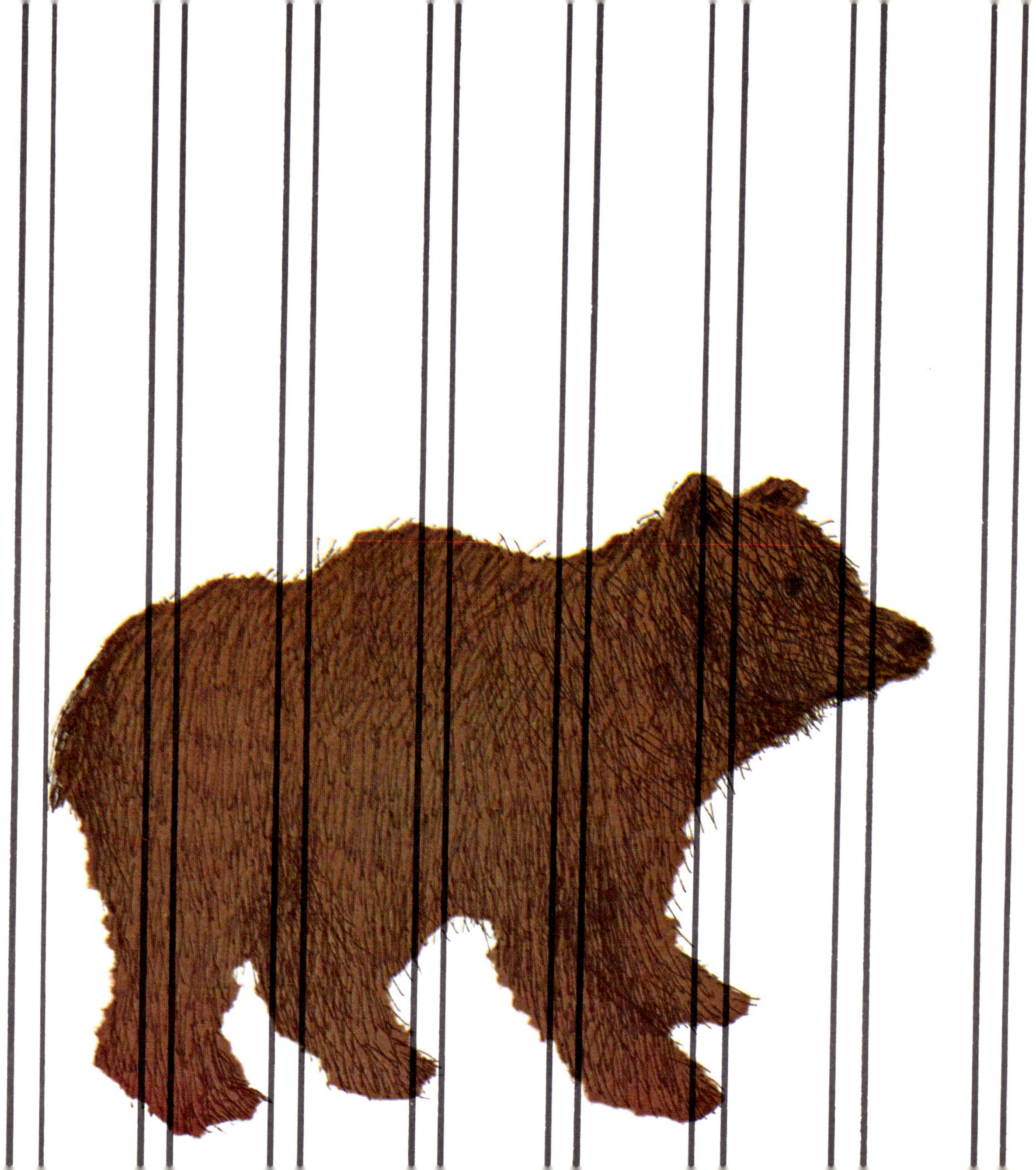

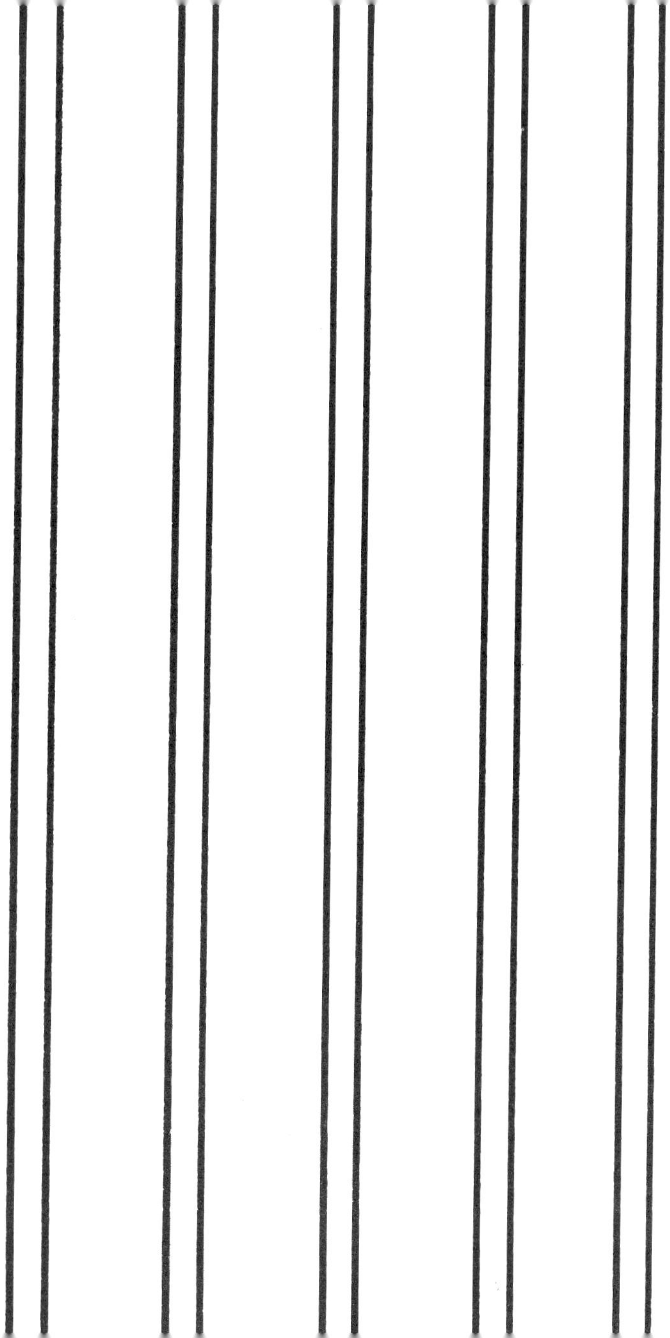

The bars of this bear's cage are parallel lines.

Slanted lines make a village of tepees.

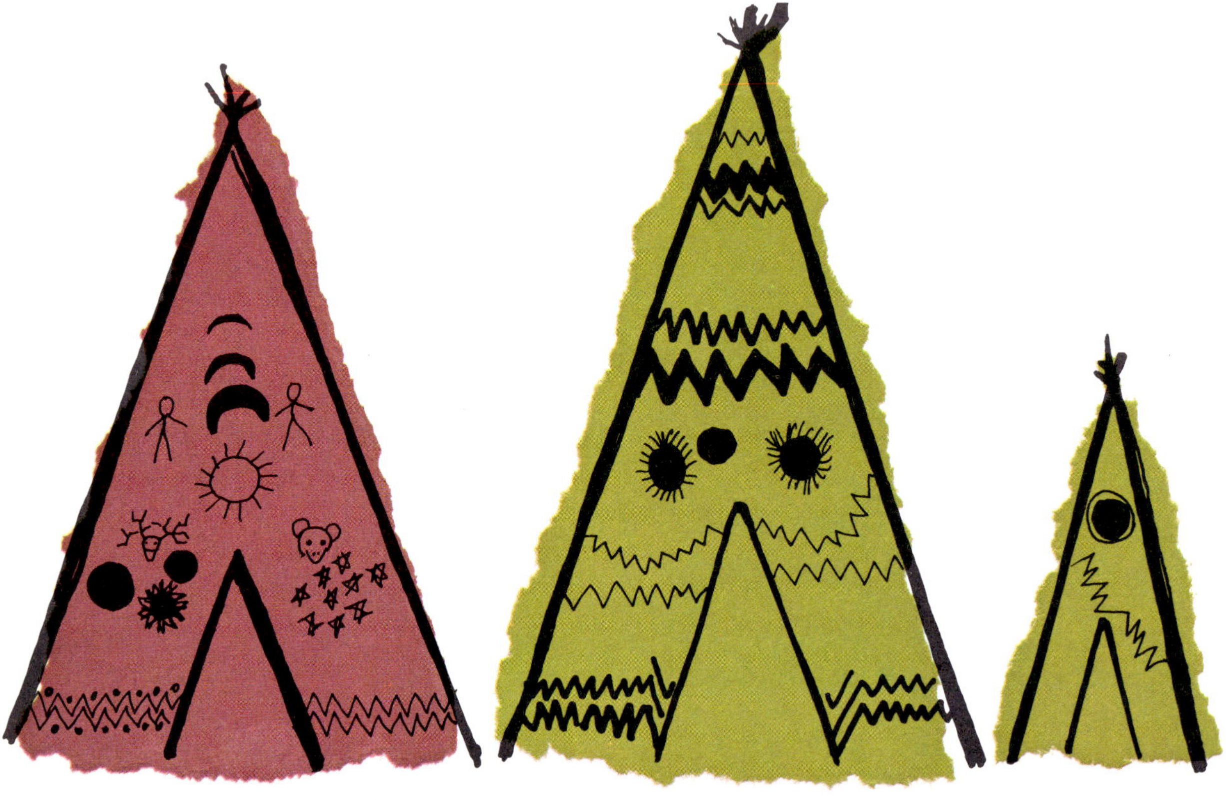

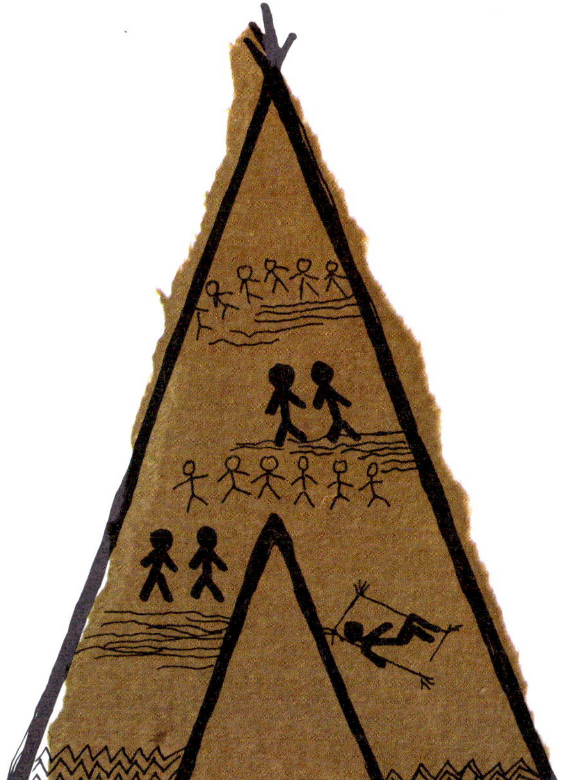

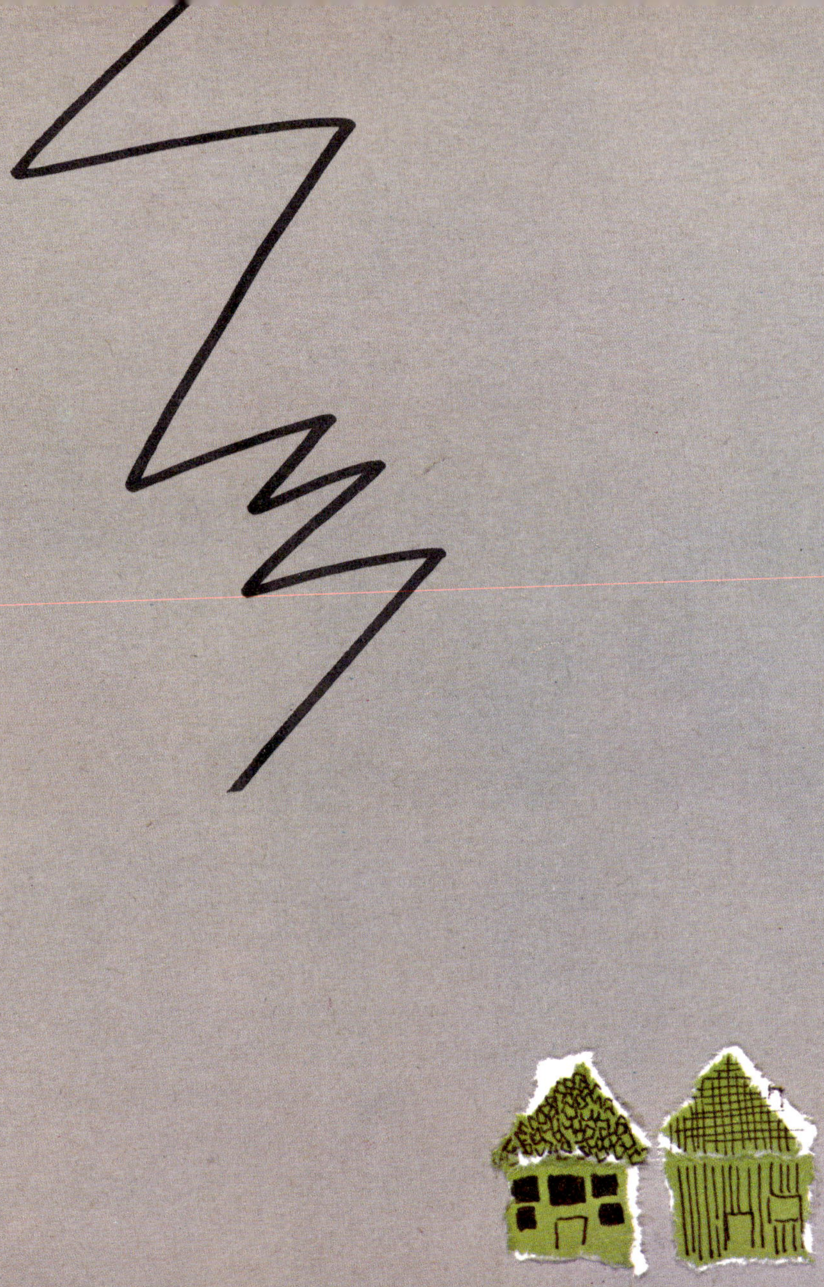

Lightning in the sky is a zigzag line.

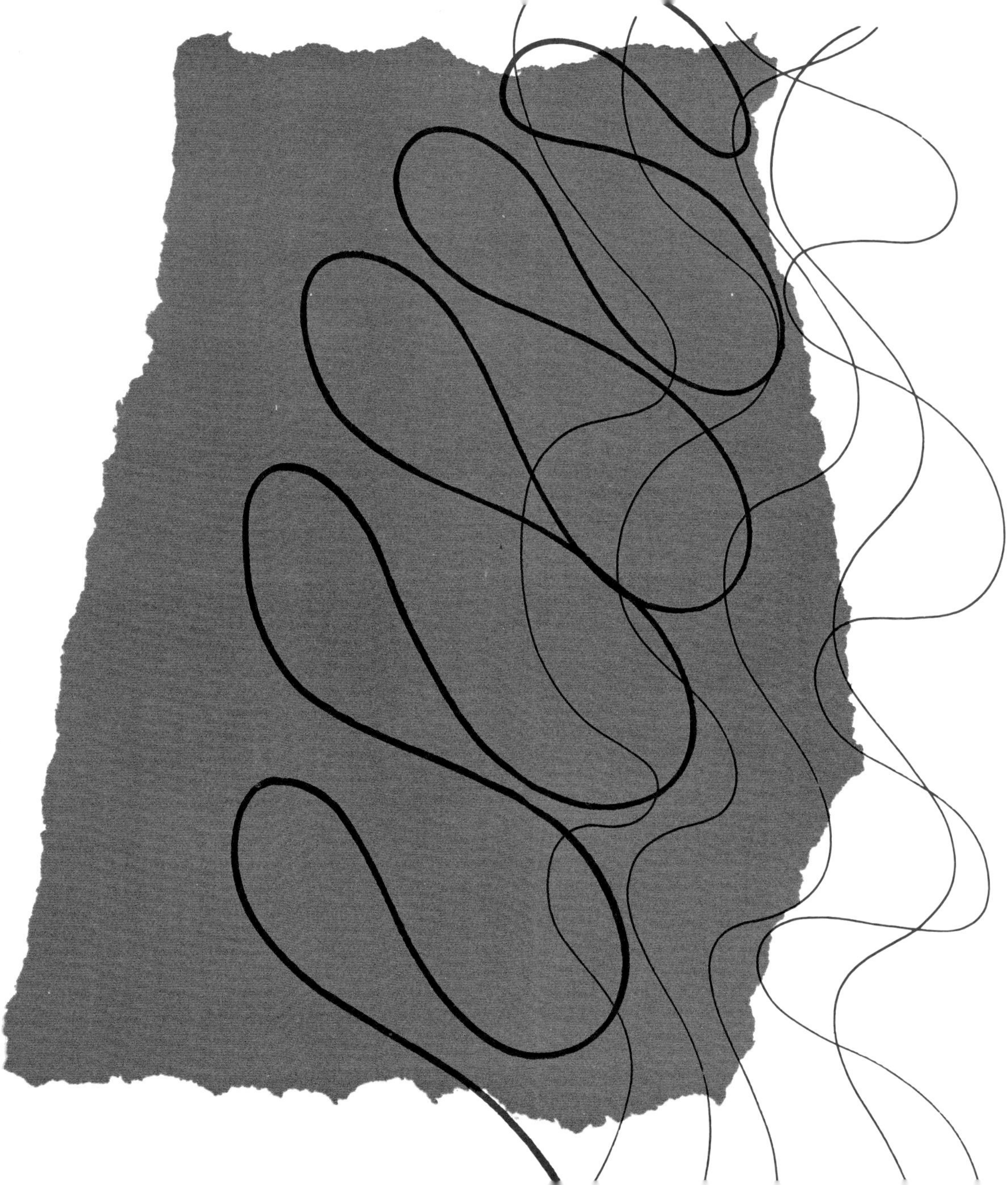

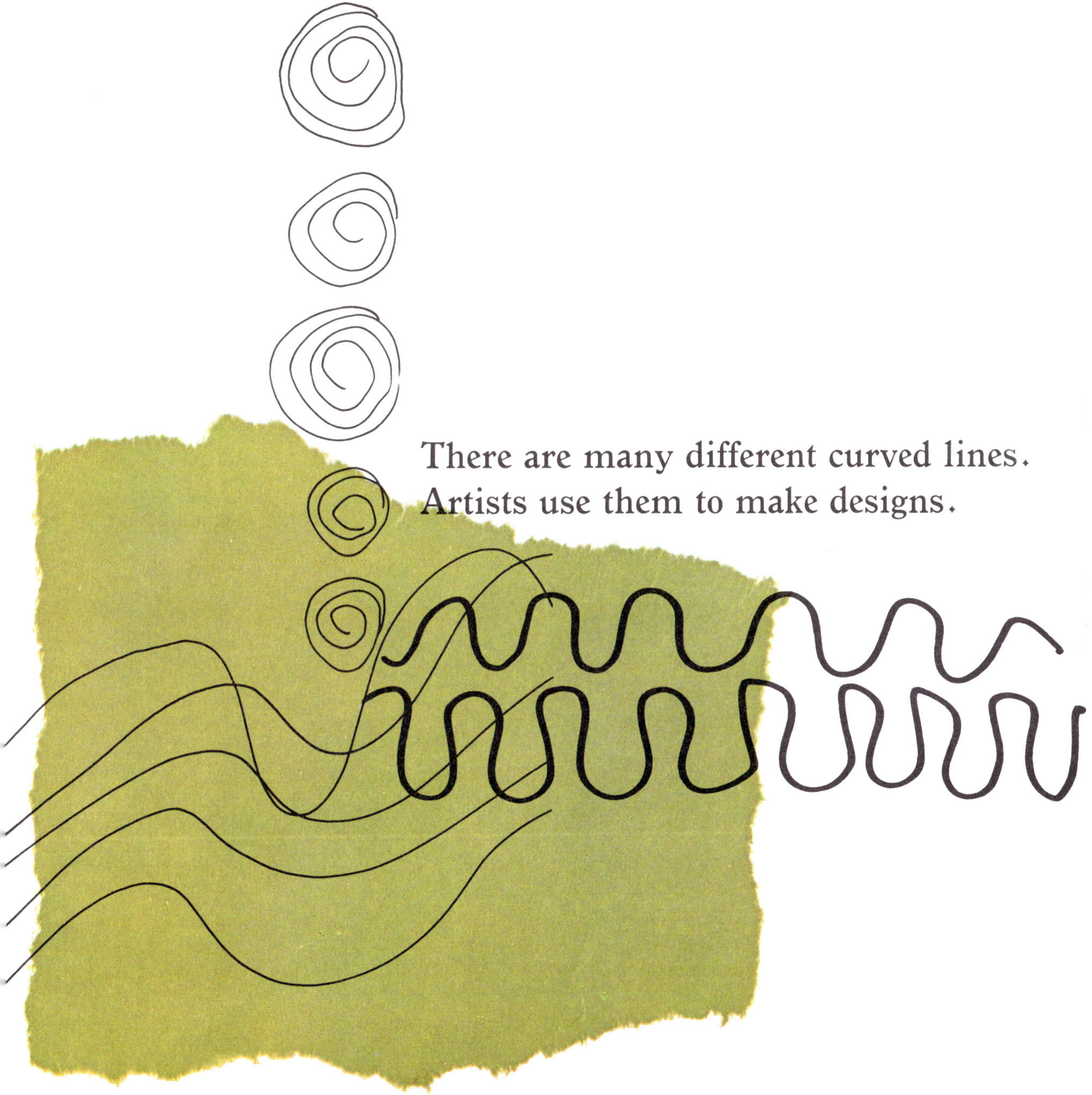

There are many different curved lines.
Artists use them to make designs.

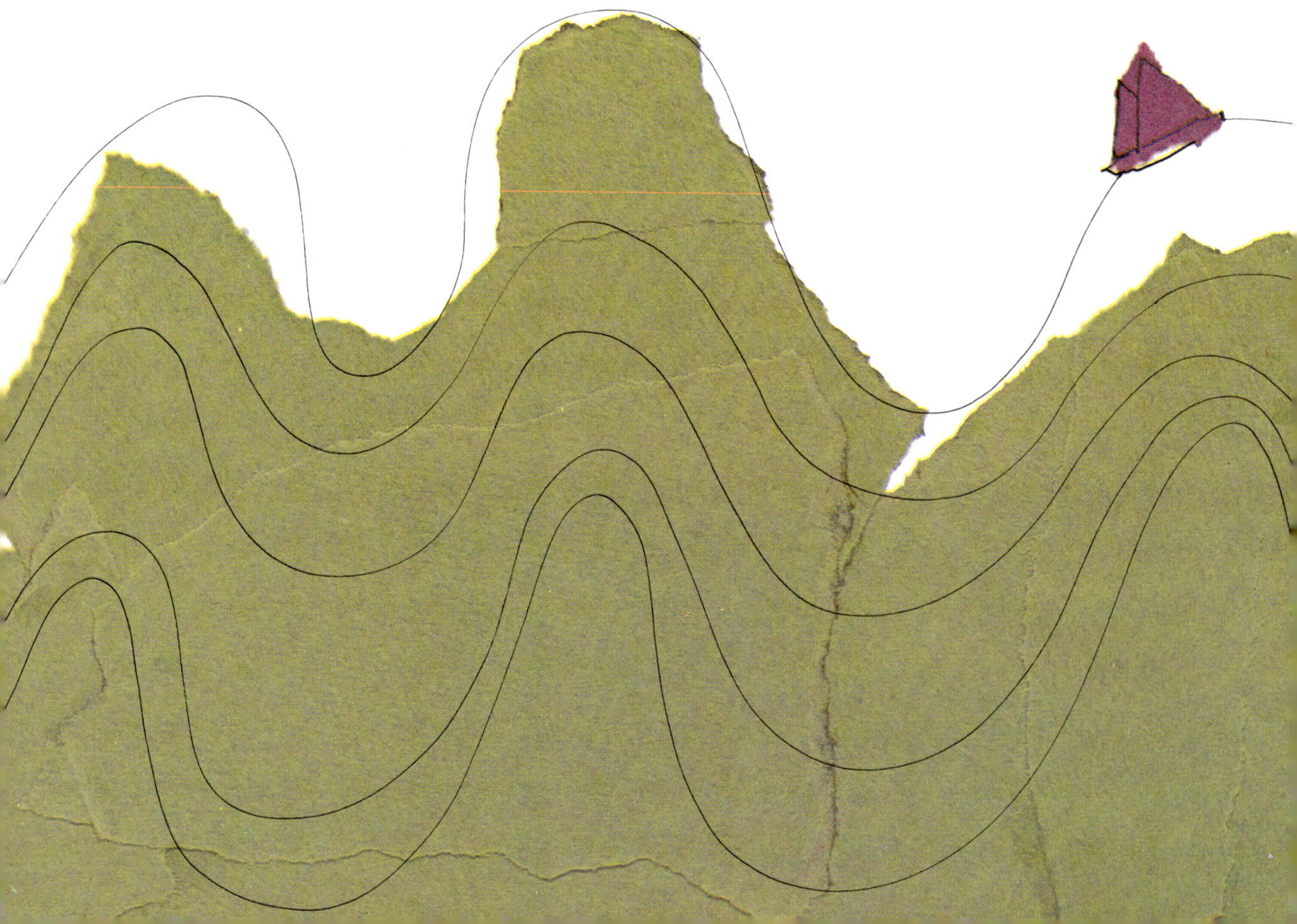

Curved lines are graceful.
They lead easily from one place to another.

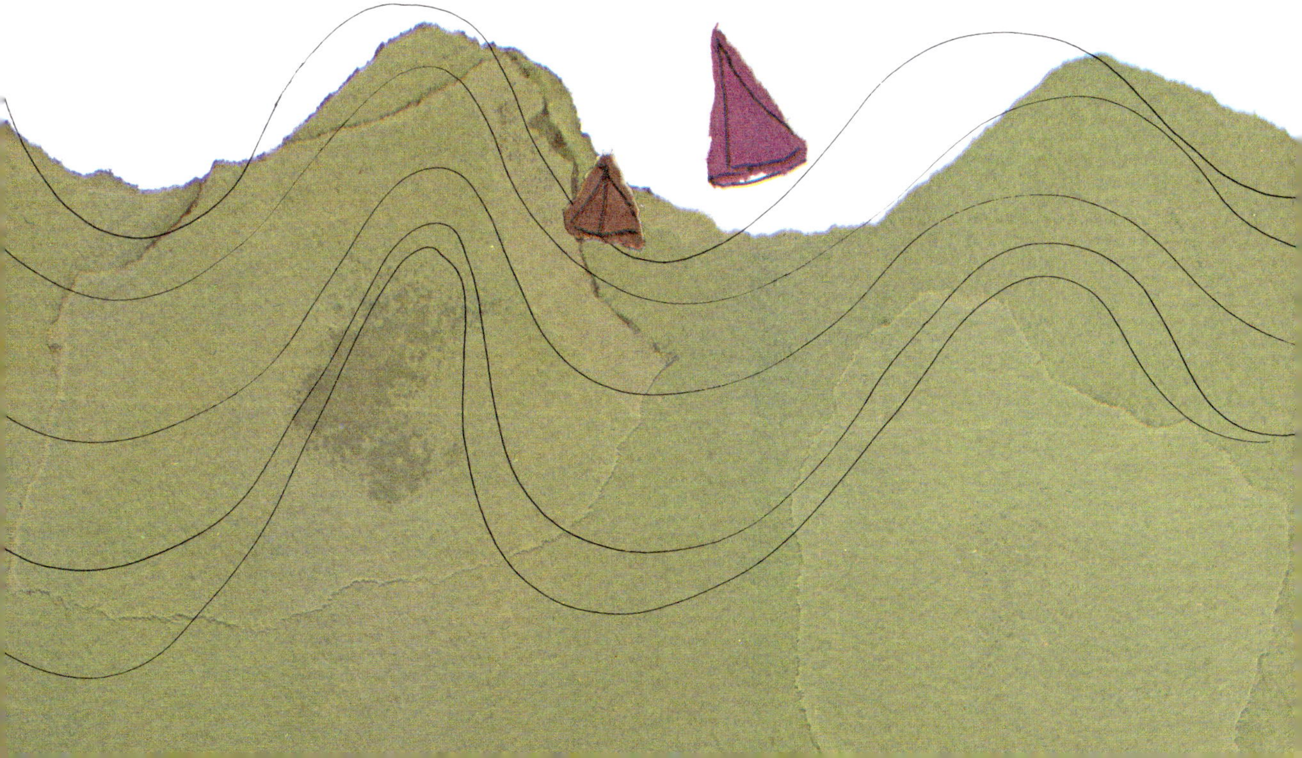

With curved lines, you can make
an O, an S, a 6 and an 8.

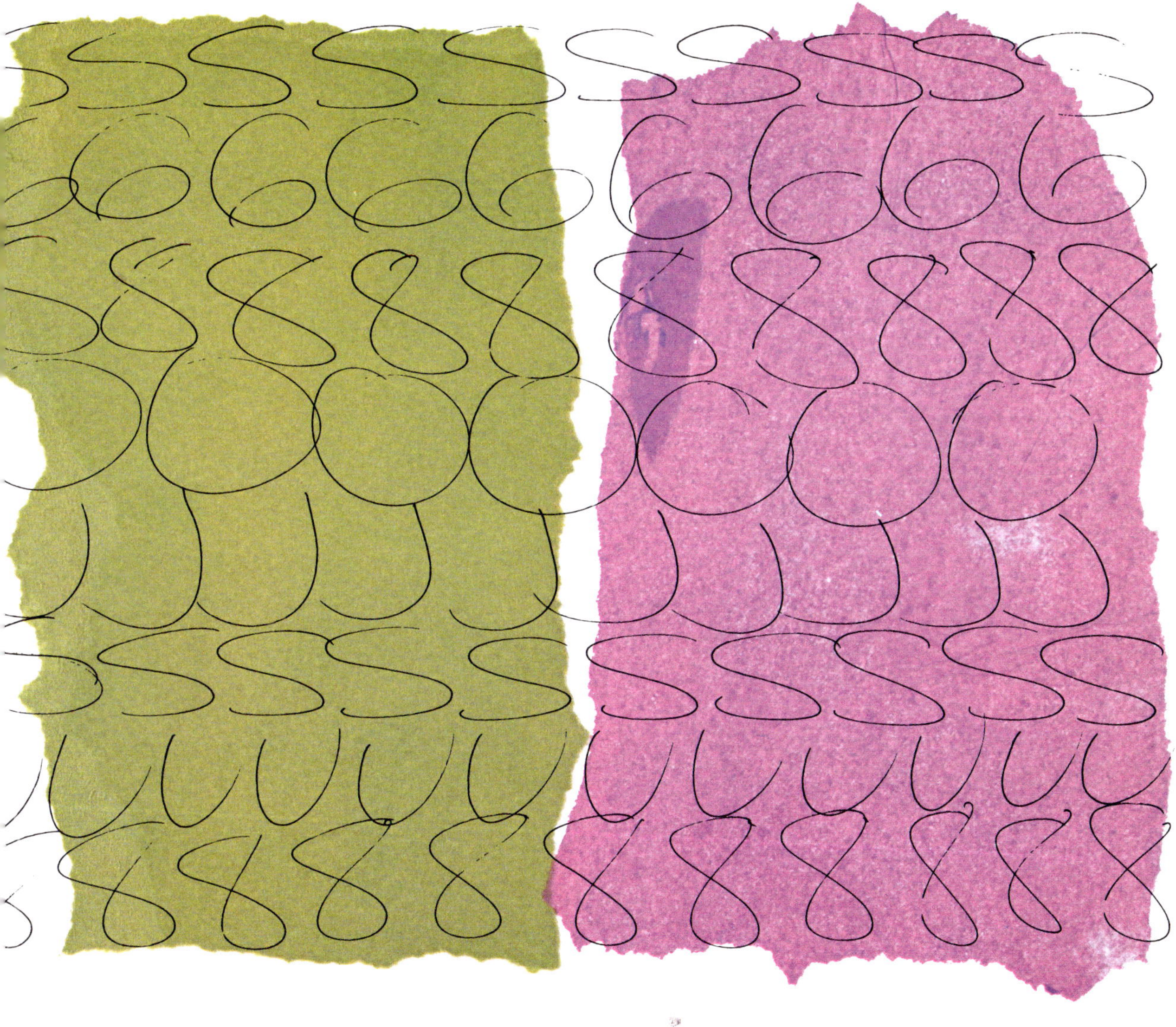

A weaving of curves makes a small bird's nest.

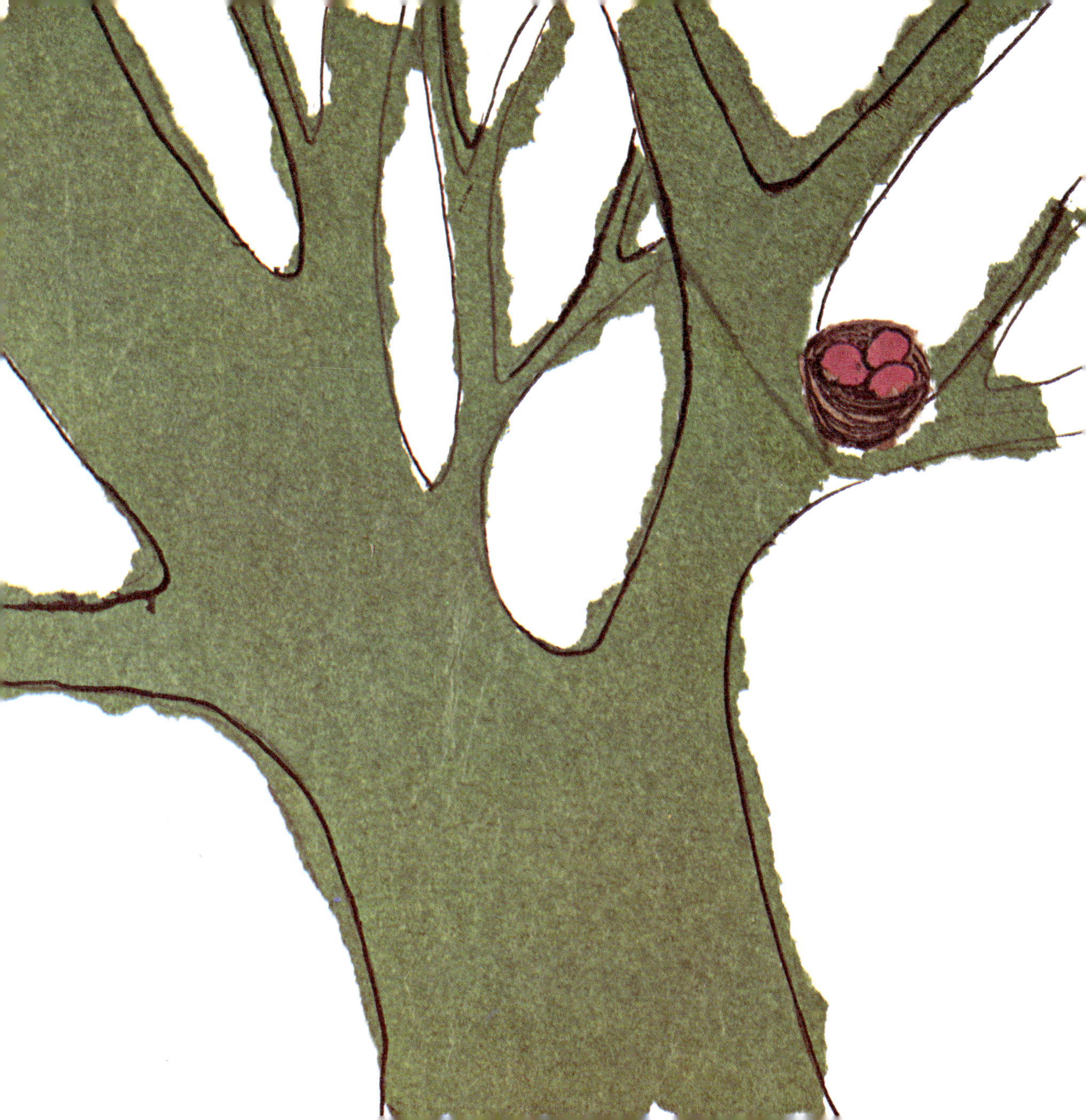

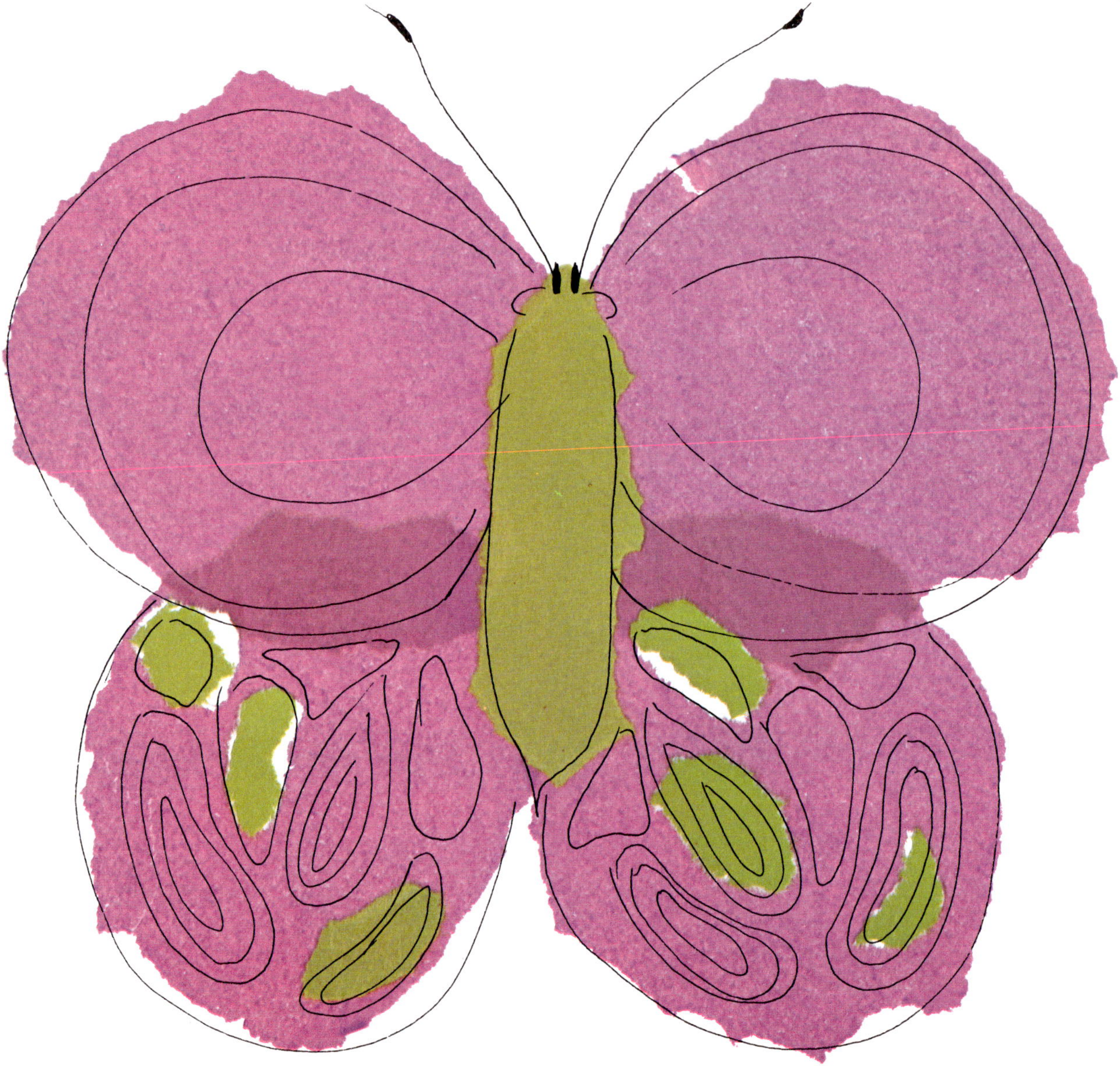

A gathering of curves makes two butterfly wings.

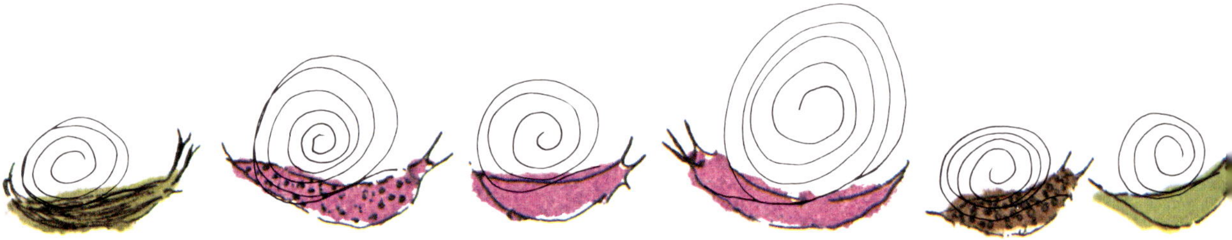

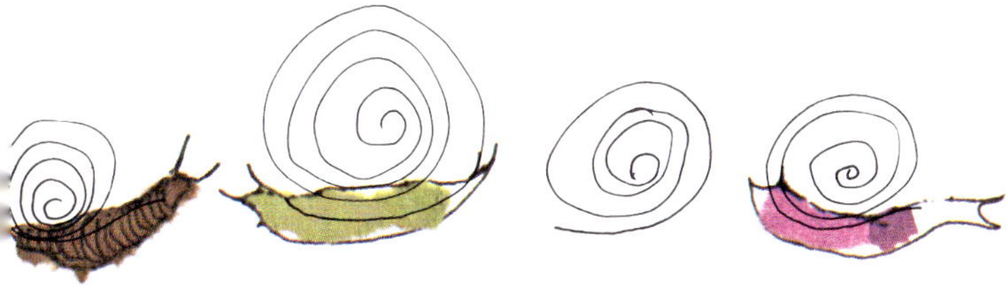

Some lines curve round
and round into spirals
like the shell of a snail.

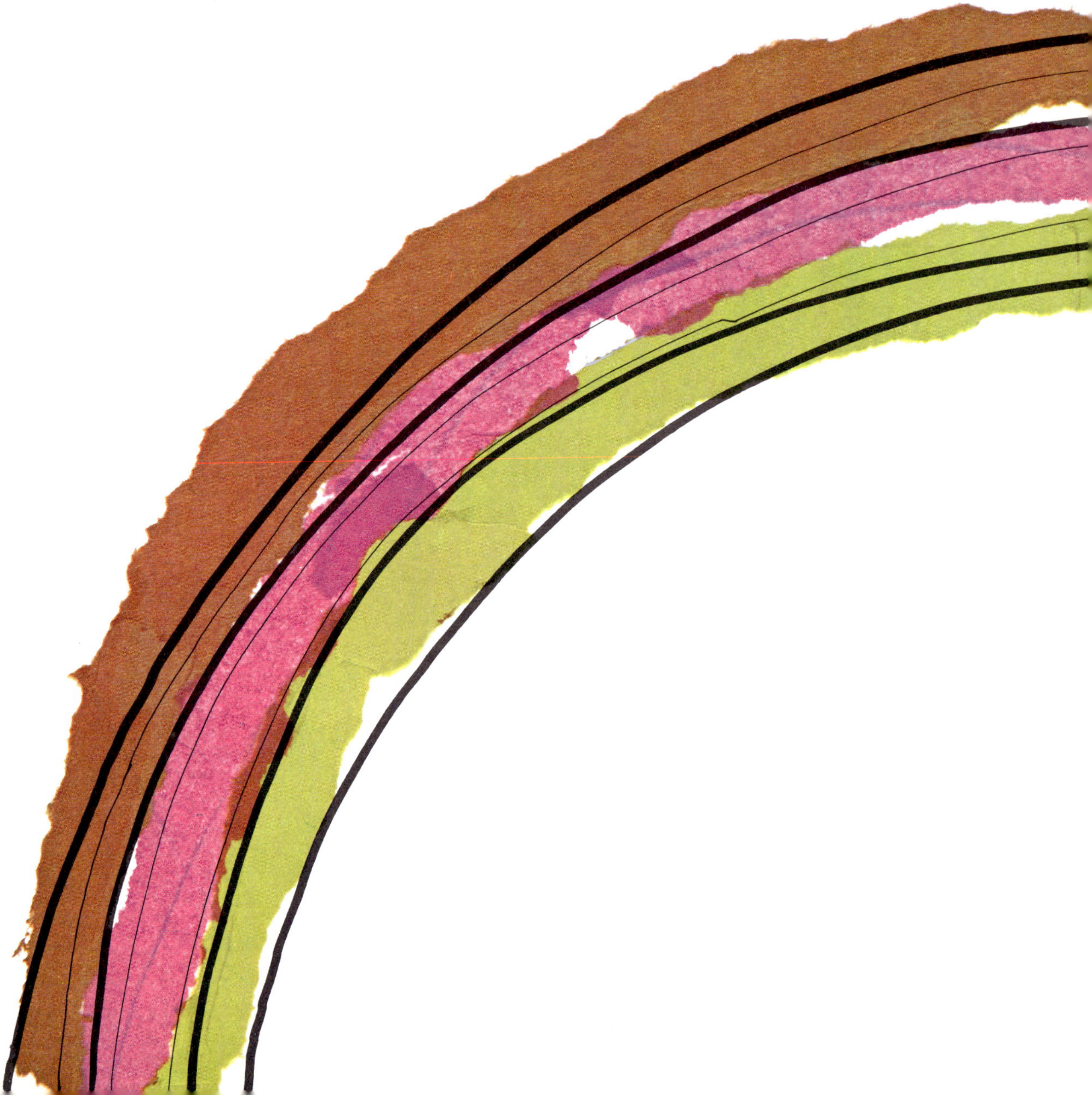

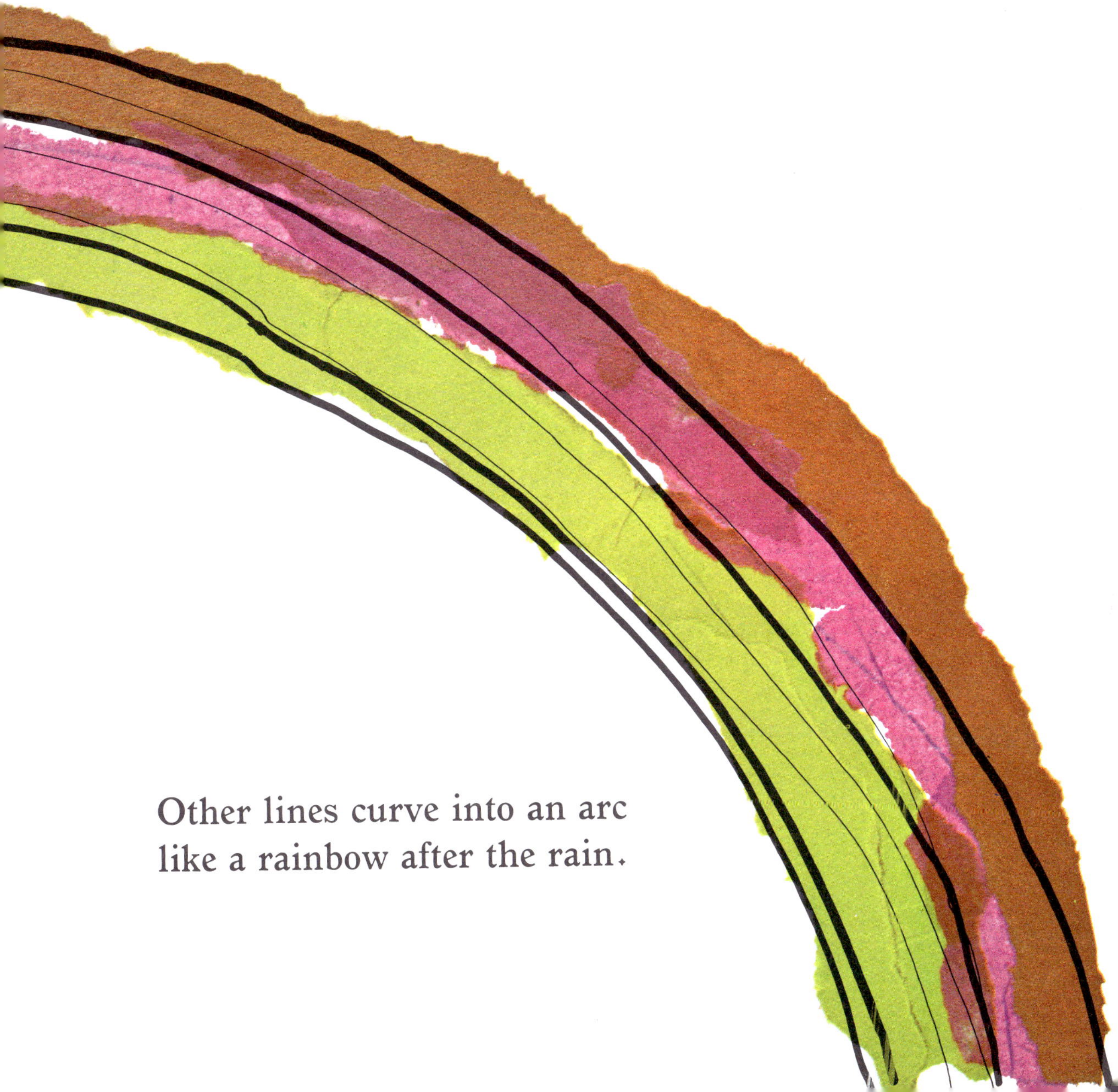

Other lines curve into an arc
like a rainbow after the rain.

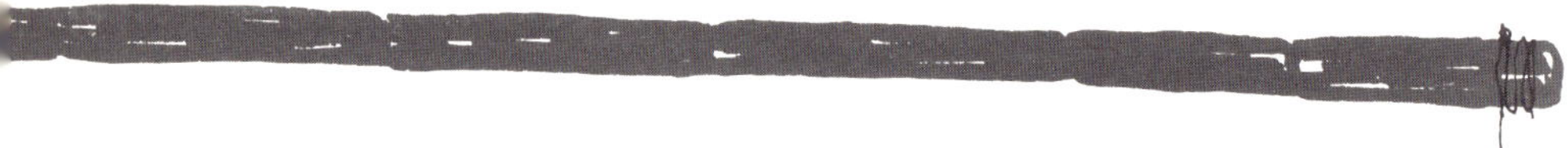

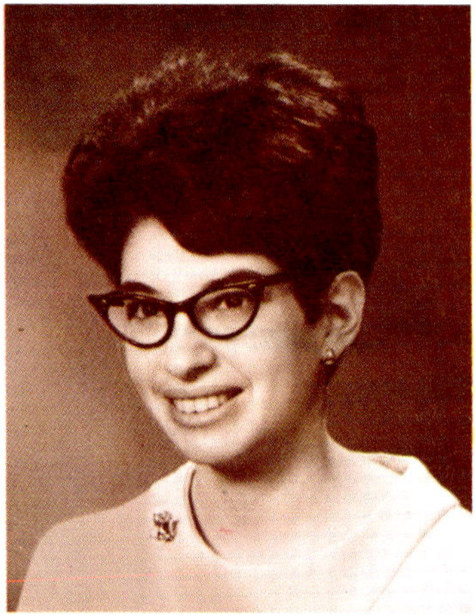

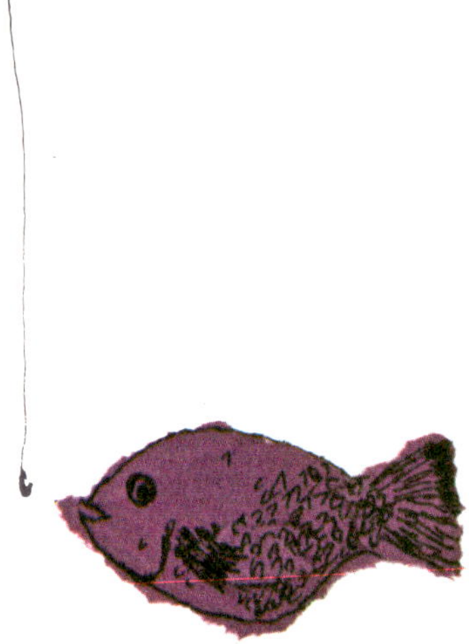

ABOUT THE AUTHOR

Sharon Lerner's published works combine her love of nature, art, and writing. As an artist, Mrs. Lerner experiments in various art forms but prefers to paint in watercolors. She has a degree in art education from the University of Minnesota and has been a lecturer and guide at the Walker Art Center and the Minneapolis Institute of Arts. She has taught at University High School, Walker Art Center and in the White Bear Public School System. An experienced writer and illustrator, Mrs. Lerner has authored or illustrated *Places of Musical Fame*, *The Self-Portrait in Art*, *I Found a Leaf*, *I Like Vegetables*, *I Like Fruit*, *I Picked a Flower*, *Who Will Wake Up Spring?*, *Orange is a Color*, *Straight is a Line*, and *Square is a Shape*. She resides in Minneapolis with her husband and children.